Pale Bloom

Pale Bloom

*A Journey of Faith,
Wounds, and Radical Grace*

ATTILA TAKACS

RESOURCE *Publications* • Eugene, Oregon

PALE BLOOM
A Journey of Faith, Wounds, and Radical Grace

Copyright © 2025 Attila Takacs. All rights reserved. Except for brief quotations in critical publications or reviews, no part of this book may be reproduced in any manner without prior written permission from the publisher. Write: Permissions, Wipf and Stock Publishers, 199 W. 8th Ave., Suite 3, Eugene, OR 97401.

Resource Publications
An Imprint of Wipf and Stock Publishers
199 W. 8th Ave., Suite 3
Eugene, OR 97401

www.wipfandstock.com

PAPERBACK ISBN: 979-8-3852-6509-1
HARDCOVER ISBN: 979-8-3852-6510-7
EBOOK ISBN: 979-8-3852-6511-4

All Scripture quotations are from the New Revised Standard Version Bible, copyright © 1989 National Council of the Churches of Christ in the United States of America. Used by permission. All rights reserved worldwide.

For my father, Gabor,
whose love was fractured, stubborn,
and still somehow held.
This remembers the man who tried
even when the world frayed him thin.

For the Unseen Father I could not see,
who sat beside a child hiding in a wardrobe,
who warmed the cold hours,
who listened to whispered stories
when no human ear cared to hear.
You were the presence beneath the silence.

For my therapist, Carrie,
who steadied the tremor in my voice,
who handed me back my own name
when I thought I'd lost it,
who walked with me until the ground
stopped shaking under my feet.

For the creatures who found me
in the years when gentleness felt unreal,
whose quiet trust and watchful eyes
taught me a wilder kind of mercy.
Their companionship was a blessing
I did not have to earn.

Contents

Acknowledgments ix
Preface x

PART I: TESTIMONY—WOUNDS AND GRACE

Early Life and Wounds 3
The Hand of Christ 7
The Search for Home 9
The Wrestling of Identity 11
The Call to Radical Grace 14
Looking Forward 17
Threads of Destiny 20

Bridge I—Interlude: Legacy 21

PART II: PROPHETIC PSALMS

No Veil Can Hide 25
No Sword, No Wall 27
The Way Is Slain 29
Given to Us 31
Christ Wept Once More 33
The True King 35
I Forgive You, Brother 37

Bridge II—Interlude: Awakening 39

Contents

PART III: CREATION AND KINSHIP

Creation Groans 43
Greening 45
Deconstruction of the Rainbow 47
Wild Folks of God 49
More than a Dog 51
Three Mothers 53
Brothers or Sisters? 55
Bond Remains 57

Bridge III—Interlude: Exiled Child 59

PART IV: LAMENT AND HEALING

Good like Fire 63
Blighted Man 65
Am I Wicked? 67
The Parent Who Waits 69
Did Anyone Ask God? 71
Black Sheep 73
Too Much Light 74

Bridge IV—Interlude: Paschal Hope 76

PART V: CONTEMPLATIVE PIECES

Beauty of Holiness 79
Spring of Life 81
Dear Love 83
Morning Watch 85
Summer Has Come 87
Harvest 89
Spark to Flame 91
Pray for a World 93

Bridge V—Interlude: Communion 95

Coda: The Last Bloom 96

Appendix: Guardrails / Mental Health Helplines 101

Acknowledgments

I WANT TO THANK my two best friends, Martin and Judith, my chosen family since primary school. You were the ones who stayed through the darkest years of Catholic abuse, when everything felt too heavy to bear alone. Your loyalty saved more of me than you know. I hope we end up old and ridiculous together in the same care home one day, playing video games and yelling at kids outside our window like gremlins with pension plans.

To my grandfather, István: Thank you for your steady kindness, your support, and your quiet, relentless generosity. You have given me stability, dignity, and the sense that I belonged somewhere in this world. I love you deeply, and I hope these pages honour even a fraction of the love you've shown me.

To my great-grandmother: You passed down the faith that shaped my father, my grandfather, and me. Even when you carried yourself like a "Vatican Princess," your heart was gold, and your devotion ran deeper than appearances. If you see this from above, I hope you are proud. And now that our long-hidden family truth has been brought into the light—that we are Ashkenazi Jews who used Catholicism to protect ourselves through dangerous generations—know this: the shame is gone. We are proud Ashkenazi Jews and Christians, and no force will make us bury our story again. May you and great-grandfather rest knowing that our name, our lineage, and our truth have been restored.

Preface

CONTENT NOTE

The pages ahead include non-graphic references to childhood abuse, suicidality, and spiritual abuse. These are not offered to shock but to bear honest witness—and to point to the mercy that broke through even there.

AUTHOR'S NOTE

A word on holy experiences: what I share here is testimony, not prescription. I do not claim the authority of prophet or ruler, nor do I seek disciples. My hope is only to point toward the One who rescued me. I invite your discernment and welcome the wisdom of those who walk faithfully ahead of me. Should anything here feel excessive, measure it by Scripture, the church's long memory, and the steady counsel of the trustworthy.

ON CHRISTIAN MYSTICISM

When I speak of being a Christian mystic, I am not claiming secret powers or rival revelations. I mean only this: to lean so deeply into prayer that Christ becomes the most solid reality. True mysticism is not flight from the world but fuller presence within it, held close to God. It adds nothing new to the faith but draws us back again to the Scriptures already given and the sacraments already entrusted.

My footsteps fall behind those of earlier pilgrims.

Francis of Assisi shed wealth to walk lightly with the gospel, until even sparrows seemed to answer his joy. Teresa of Ávila mapped prayer like a many-chambered castle, showing that God is not distant but waits in the innermost room. Hildegard of Bingen, abbess and artist, sang creation alive with divine fire.

They remind me what real mysticism is: humility instead of spectacle, nearness instead of novelty. To seek Christ so fully that one returns bearing mercy, wisdom, and courage. This, too, is why I write—not to dazzle but to share fragile blooms of grace that may point toward his Presence.

Part I:
Testimony—Wounds and Grace

Early Life and Wounds

I WAS BORN INTO a faith that should have been a shelter. Ours was a traditional Catholic home, threaded with my Ashkenazi Jewish roots—heritage carried in blood and memory, even when hidden by incense and Latin. From the outside it looked devout; on the inside it often felt cold and perfectionist, the kind of religion that measured before it embraced. I learned the motions early: stand, kneel, recite. But a child needs more than choreography. A child needs arms.

Too young, I learned betrayal by people who were meant to protect me. Some wore religious clothes; some were family. I will not linger on details, but those years put deep cracks in me. When adults misuse authority in God's name, it does not only wound the body; it twists the compass. You don't know which way is north anymore, and shame follows you into sleep. "The LORD is near to the brokenhearted, and saves the crushed in spirit" (Ps 34:18).

Beneath the churchly surface another current ran—gnostic, though I had no word for it then. Gnosticism—ancient or modern—whispers of secret ladders only a few may climb. It borrows Christian words and flips them, like a cross in a mirror. Rituals that should have carried freedom felt watched, hedged, transactional, as if the invisible world were a market where power could be bartered. It did not set captives free. It fed fear. It taught me to confuse holiness with performance and God with a code to be cracked.

I adapted. Independence kept me alive, but it is a poor blanket on cold nights. Beneath it lay another truth: the ache for a mother's

Part I: Testimony—Wounds and Grace

warmth, for a steady hand to say, "You are safe here." To survive, my soul built a guardian inside me—what a therapist might call a trauma adaptation—refusing to let the child I was be abandoned. That inner guard helped me live through things no child should face. But a sentinel is not a savior.

By twelve the pain had ripened into despair. I was exhausted from surviving. I will not recount the method, only the moment: I decided I could not bear another day—and Jesus stepped in. Not an idea, not a myth, but a Person. A warmth like a hand, firm and undeniable, stopping the unthinkable. I had not gone looking for him; he came looking for me. In the darkest room of my life, the Light arrived uninvited and would not let me die. "Even though I walk through the darkest valley, I fear no evil; for you are with me" (Ps 23:4).

That night, sleep broke open.

I stood in a place like our world, but the sky was pure light—bright without burning. A boy my age stood before me. His clothing seemed woven of light that shifted and blended into the air; from the shoulders he faded toward brightness like watercolor in water. I could not speak. He alone could.

"My time is short," he said. "Listen. Your suffering has been seen. You will be liberated from the wicked hands of your captors. It is decided. It is written, and no sorcerer can undo it. A chance will come sooner than you expect. Hold it and do not let go until you are safe from the darkness. You will be tempted to turn back and search their faces—asking if they can change, if they can love you, if you can heal them. You are a child, and their pain has consumed them. They are beyond your help. They require another help. Only living water can do that now. You must leave. Your life depends on it."

He fell silent and studied my face. Then, softly, "Be careful, Atty." A single tear slid from his right eye.

It felt as if a hand struck my chest. My voice returned and I blurted, "I know who you are." Everything shifted. I woke on my bed with one tear on my right cheek, the same as his. I cannot certify it—only confess that in the vision I knew him, and on waking

I trusted his genuineness more than his name. I brought that to prayer and testing. What remained was the word that mattered: leave, live, and do not try to save with your own strength what only the living water can heal (see John 4:14). Scripture says, "Test everything; hold fast to what is good" (1 Thess 5:21). I did not take this experience as unquestionable. I weighed it with prayer, with Scripture open before me, and in conversation with wiser voices than mine. What endured was not the strangeness of the moment but its fruit: it gave me courage to leave danger, clarity to stop bargaining with abusers, and a deeper trust in Christ's mercy. That fruit was enough.

None of this was casual. Christ did not wander by and rescue me on a whim. He cut through a thicket of lies and fear and the gnostic bargain that had stalked my childhood. He refused the market of power and met me with mercy. Where secrecy tried to bind me, he spoke plainly. Where a counterfeit promised control, he offered presence. Where death opened its mouth, he closed it.

I am not a prophet, nor do I wish to be. I submit this experience to Scripture and to the wise counsel of tested pastors and therapists. I tell it as a witness to what God did for one frightened child—nothing more, nothing less. Power gathers crowds; my heroes—Francis, Hildegard, Teresa—knelt in humility, seeking union with Christ so they could return and tend the people, not rule them. If you are wary, judge this by its fruit: Did it bring me to safety, repentance, and deeper love for Christ? If yes, receive it as testimony; if not, leave it by the roadside.

Visions and dreams are not new revelation. At their best, they are echoes that lead us back to the word already spoken in Christ. If an experience magnifies Jesus, calls for repentance, and bears the fruit of love, then it can be kept as testimony. If it does not, it should be set aside. This one, for me, was not about power but about rescue.

That encounter did not erase the past, but it redrew the map. I knew—beneath doctrine and ritual—that there is a Shepherd who sees, who knows, who interrupts death. From that day I carried a quiet certainty: if everyone else fails, Christ will not. I did not

Part I: Testimony—Wounds and Grace

yet understand grace, but I had met the One who gives it. And once you have met him, you cannot unknow him. Even when you wander, he remains.

This is where my story begins—not with my wounds, not with the darkness that named itself a savior, but with the One who refused to let my wounds have the last word.

The Hand of Christ

AFTER THAT NIGHT AT twelve, I did not wake into safety. The same faces, the same rooms, the same memories that pricked like glass under the skin remained. But something had changed in me: I knew I was not alone. The Presence that stopped me did not leave when the crisis passed. He stayed.

At first his nearness came as simple instructions at the edge of my thoughts: breathe . . . step . . . wait . . . don't answer that voice. I didn't yet have a prayer life; I had a lifeline. When shame rose like a tide, I remembered the warmth of that hand and prayed a single sentence—sometimes only his name—and the tide receded enough for me to stand. This was my first lesson in grace: not a concept to master but a Person who holds you when you cannot hold yourself. "My grace is sufficient for you, for power is made perfect in weakness" (2 Cor 12:9).

He cut pathways where none existed. A book fell open to the line I needed. A stranger spoke an answer I hadn't dared to ask out loud. In heavy places he taught me to be simple and stubborn: "Jesus, have mercy." I was not defeating darkness; I was refusing its terms. He did the rest.

The institutions around me did not become sudden allies. Rules often sounded louder than mercy. Yet even there, Christ gave small kindnesses: a kind face in a cold room, a hymn that cracked the shell around my heart, a moment at the back of a church where tears came without shame. He was like water finding the lowest places—quiet, patient, faithful. "A bruised reed he will not break, and a dimly burning wick he will not quench" (Isa 42:3).

Part I: Testimony—Wounds and Grace

He began to retrain my instincts. Survival had taught me to harden, to trust no one, to keep moving. Christ taught me a harder courage: to be soft without breaking; to tell the truth without becoming a blade; to forgive without pretending evil is small. He never romanticized my pain; he shouldered it. When I could not carry the cross, he carried it with me.

Of course there were setbacks. Some days I felt I had unlearned nothing. Triggers flashed; sleep fled; the old scripts returned: You are alone. You are dirty. You are not worth saving. But grace had planted a contradiction inside me. A new script spoke back: You are mine. I chose you. I will finish what I began. "I am confident of this, that the one who began a good work among you will bring it to completion by the day of Jesus Christ" (Phil 1:6). I learned to live between those voices—and to side with the One who had proven himself with a hand between me and the blade.

I cannot map the theology of it as neatly as some would like. I only know this: Christ's companionship became the truest fact of my days. When leaders failed, he didn't. When churches argued, he listened. When I was too tired to be brave, he lent me his courage. Slowly, almost without noticing, I began to believe that healing was not a fantasy for other people. It was a road I was already walking—one step, one breath, one whispered prayer at a time.

The Search for Home

MY FIRST RELIGION WORE a Hungarian face. Beneath it ran a shadow current—whispers of secret ladders, ritual without warmth, power bartered like a commodity. I learned early that people called "holy" could harm you and still name it love.

At thirteen, grace pushed the door open. Not luck—providence. God drew me out of the hands that harmed me and set me on a new beginning in Scotland. I arrived skin and bone, with a small suitcase and a stunned heart. There, in a land I barely knew, I was reunited with my father—the man from whom that world had kept me apart. It felt as if God reached into the tangled roots of my life and pulled up one thread of mercy.

Scotland was different—less religious on the surface, more blunt about unbelief. People didn't pretend as much. They worked, worried, and got on with it. In that plain air I tried to learn a new kind of breathing. I wanted to heal from the rough hands of the "church" I had known, and from the darker forces behind it. I wanted to believe again without flinching.

But pain does not vanish when you cross a border. In classrooms and corridors I carried it with me. I still loved the Lion of Judah and clung to him like a plank in open water. Yet hatred grew in me—hatred for churches, for collars and committees, for any institution that spoke of God but did not look like him. I told myself I was done with them all. The irony wasn't lost on me: the more I swore I loved Christ, the more my anger dragged me from his voice.

Part I: Testimony—Wounds and Grace

Part of that anger was historical. As I learned Scotland's stories—towns emptied by closures, mines and factories shut, communities stripped of work and dignity—I kept asking, Where was the church? Where were the shepherds when the flock lost its pasture? "Woe to the shepherds who destroy and scatter the sheep of my pasture!" (Jer 23:1). Too often I saw polite distance or internal squabbles dressed as theology. The failure wasn't only doctrinal; it was practical. If the gospel is truly "good news to the poor" (Luke 4:18), why did so many poor say it never reached them?

Those questions hardened my suspicion. I could forgive my own wounds more easily than I could forgive the church's absence in other people's suffering. My anger felt righteous—and sometimes it was. But anger is a poor compass. It points to what's wrong; it doesn't tell you where to go. In the quiet, Christ kept tugging: Don't mistake their failures for mine. He would not let me confuse his heart with their history.

I didn't yet know where home would be. Catholicism felt like a scar. That shadow current of secrecy and control was a door I would never touch again. Scotland's churches looked tired or compromised, and I was weary of disappointment. But the Shepherd had not left. Even as I pushed away, he stayed close—patient, unoffended, firm. He let me ask hard questions. He let me grieve what was lost in Hungary and what was neglected in Scotland. And he kept the search alive: not for a perfect institution but for a people who would love truth and grace at the same time.

The road ran through new doors—Episcopalian ritual, evangelical fire—through fresh disappointments and surprising mercies. But one thing was settled: I was done with games. I was looking for Christ, and wherever he breathed freedom, I would follow.

The Wrestling of Identity

GROWING UP, I KNEW I was attracted to men. I didn't choose it; it was simply there, like being right-handed. What I did choose was to follow Jesus. Holding those two truths together felt almost impossible in most church rooms I entered. In some places I was told I was disgusting. In others, to wave a flag and stop asking questions. Neither side seemed interested in my soul.

Trauma complicates identity. Long before I had words for it, my heart grew its own guardian—a tender, protective strength that rose up whenever I was in danger. It wasn't a second self; it was survival. Later, when pain grew louder and the wider culture offered ready labels, that inner guardian made "non-binary" feel like a possible home. It promised relief: you don't have to be one thing; you can be anything. For a while, I wore that word like a bandage.

But bandages aren't skin. What I needed wasn't a new label; I needed healing. God opened a door through a trauma-wise therapist who was willing to go there with me. She didn't mock my faith. She didn't rush me. Together we traced the lines—abuse, secrecy, the gnostic shadow behind my religion, the ache for a mother's arms, the survival instinct that kept me alive. Slowly the fog thinned. I realized, for me, I wasn't non-binary and I wasn't trans. I was a man whom God carried through storms. Part of his carrying included a fierce compassion formed in me for the sake of survival. That compassion was a gift. The label I used for a season was not my home.

This didn't make me anti-people. It made me patient with people. I understand why slogans can feel like salvation when your

Part I: Testimony — Wounds and Grace

world is on fire. I also understand how condemnation can crush someone who is barely standing. Christ offered me a third way: radical grace joined to truth. He didn't ask me to deny reality; he asked me to walk with him in it—honestly, obediently, one step at a time. "If any want to become my followers, let them deny themselves and take up their cross daily and follow me" (Luke 9:23).

Being gay and Christian still raises hard questions—about holiness and desire, about chastity and friendship, about what the cross asks of me. I don't pretend those are easy. But I no longer let culture, left or right, do my thinking for me. I belong to Jesus. He is not ashamed of me, and he is not permissive with me. He loves me too much to lie, and too much to leave. I chose celibacy at twenty—not to impress any church but in obedience to God the Father who calls me beloved. Four years on, I keep this path because my first work is to find a spiritual home and let Christ heal my trauma. I would have made the same choice if I were straight; restoration is restoration. Desire still rises—I am human—but when it does, I remember how much healing the Spirit has grown while I've kept my closest bonds within friendship and family.

I often feel between worlds. In some LGBTQ+ spaces, sexual bravado can be loud; in some church rooms, rigidity can be cold. I refuse both. Scripture leaves real space for chaste, affectionate friendship—John, "the disciple whom Jesus loved" (John 13:23), resting against Jesus at supper—without forcing modern categories onto it. Men can be soul-friends without sex. Lust—gay or straight—turns people into objects; love honors persons. For now, I embrace celibacy and chaste fellowship, entrusting my desires to Jesus. I do not claim this settles every debate. It is simply the honest road I can walk before the Lord who knows me. When he redirects me, I will follow; until then, I will keep choosing the narrow way that is bringing me to life. "Enter through the narrow gate; for the gate is wide and the road is easy that leads to destruction. . . . For the gate is narrow and the road is hard that leads to life" (Matt 7:13–14).

The therapy room taught me something the church should have taught me sooner: not every feeling is an identity, not every label is liberation, and not every question is rebellion. Sometimes a question is the first honest prayer. When I lifted mine, Jesus answered—not with a new tribe to join but with himself. He showed me my protective tenderness wasn't a mistake; it was a mercy he repurposed. He showed me my worth isn't measured by a banner, a hashtag, or a committee vote, but by the scars in his hands.

So I laid the bandage down. I stepped out of the fog—not into someone else's camp but into the clearer air where Christ stands. I am a man, loved by God, called to holiness, carrying both courage and compassion. My desires don't define me. My past doesn't doom me. My labels don't save me. Jesus does.

The Call to Radical Grace

SOME CHURCHES WIELD TRUTH like a weapon; others thin it until it no longer matters. I have stood between those fires long enough to know that neither saves. Militant religion shouts with swords—correct in words, perhaps, but loveless, leaving people bleeding on the steps. Political religion smiles politely—kind in tone, perhaps, but weightless, blessing whatever the age demands. Both betray the gospel because both refuse the cross.

The cross is not a prop. It is where mercy and justice meet without compromise. Radical grace does not deny sin; it names it and then stays to bind the wound. It refuses the lie that love is license and the lie that holiness is hatred. Grace is not soft because it avoids the wound; it is strong because it tends it, day after day, until healing takes root. "The law indeed was given through Moses; grace and truth came through Jesus Christ" (John 1:17).

I learned this slowly. Militant preaching could make me cheer for a moment, then leave me colder—angry, armed, and secretly afraid. Soft religion could make me feel seen yet never told me how to live—no cross, no call, no change. Radical grace does something different. It looks you in the eye and says, You are loved. Now repent. Come, walk with me. It strips away pretense—left and right, rebel and Pharisee—and returns us to the narrow road where Christ is both Shepherd and Lord.

I once saw this lived in the priest who baptized me, Father Gyula. He pushed a parish to feed a starving single mother. He remembered faces years after baptizing them. When a young man—barely nineteen, back from university, ashamed and spent on parties, beds, and weed—slipped into the back pew, Father Gyula took his shaking hand: "You are home. Jesus loves you with a true heart. Keep coming. We'll walk this road together." When critics muttered that he was sentimental or soft on sin, he answered quietly, "Wolves bite. A shepherd protects." Then he did the harder work: met the boy for coffee, helped him make amends, and taught him how repentance becomes a path, not a slogan. That is radical grace in a collar: truth that guards, love that costs.

Radical grace is practical. It does not end in slogans. It visits the single mother choosing between rent and dinner. It remembers the men who lost their work when the mines closed and helps them find dignity again. It feeds, listens, teaches, and—when necessary—stands before rulers to say, "You are harming the flock." It is neither a grant-chasing NGO nor a war camp hunting enemies. It is a people carrying one another's crosses while following the Man of Sorrows who carried ours. "Bear one another's burdens, and in this way you will fulfill the law of Christ" (Gal 6:2).

This path refuses two easy errors. First, cruelty disguised as zeal. Truth without love makes liars of us; we preach a holy God with unholy hearts. Second, cowardice disguised as kindness. Love without truth makes cowards of us; we preach a kind God who never asks anyone to change. Christ is not half of either; he is fullness. To the woman caught in sin he says, "Neither do I condemn you. Go your way, and from now on do not sin again" (John 8:11). He welcomes enemies and makes them friends—but on his terms, not ours.

Repentance, then, is surgery: remove what festers so you can walk. Holiness is the recovery that follows. Self-denial is not self-hatred; it is making room for the life of Christ, stronger and more tender than ours. The cross is not a posture; it is a daily choice to follow Love where he leads, even uphill.

This is the road I want to walk and the road I invite others onto—not with threats, not with flattery, but with the quiet courage of people who have been forgiven. Radical grace does not compromise with idols, whatever flag they fly. It tells the truth, lays down its life, and keeps its arms open. It is slower than outrage and

Part I: Testimony—Wounds and Grace

quieter than branding, but it endures. And when we live it, people do not meet our tribe—they meet Jesus.

Looking Forward

FOR A TIME I lived between two doors: evangelical fire and Episcopalian rhythm. I needed both—the courage to hold Scripture without apology and the quiet beauty of symbol and sacrament. In the end I put on evangelical colors—not because they are flawless but because in this season their insistence on the word steadies me. I still carry a love for liturgy; I don't want controversy to drown the beauty of worship. I am not called to a tribe so much as to a Person. "For no one can lay any foundation other than the one that has been laid; that foundation is Jesus Christ" (1 Cor 3:11). Whatever light I have glimpsed in prayer or vision, I submit it to Holy Scripture and the church's historic witness. If I am mistaken, let wiser brothers and sisters correct me; if anything in me is true, let it serve Christ alone.

One Sunday after I preached, people milled about the high school hall we hire for services. I sat quietly, replaying a conversation with a kind member who had listened to my story of abuse with real compassion. Then she urged me—warmly and repeatedly—toward the prayer circles, promising how much they had helped her in grief. I'm glad prayer held her; it should. But I am wary when prayer is used as a shortcut. God isn't a dispenser. In Scripture the Lord shows doors—and then calls us to walk: "I have set before you life and death. . . . Choose life" (Deut 30:19). Prayer is power, not magic; "faith by itself, if it has no works, is dead" (Jas 2:17).

As my anger rose—righteous maybe, but hot—a warmth pressed it down and stood me upright. At the open door of the

Part I: Testimony—Wounds and Grace

hall I sensed a quiet pull. I followed, feeling foolish to chase a thing only my soul could see. Step by step, up the High Street, it drew me to a church by the old hotel. The pull stopped; I looked up.

My local Catholic church. Flashbacks hit hard, as they always did when I faced a Catholic door. I said aloud (thank God no one was near), "You're either a genius or insane, Father. Maybe both." I noted the parish number and called. Providence met me on the line. Father M. was driving home from a study break in Spain—he was returning as I was returning. We agreed to speak after Friday Mass. It was my first local Mass in ten years. Sitting there, every nerve awake, I wondered if I'd bolt. The conversation afterward surprised me: hard, but human—mercy without denial, truth without theatrics. Something in Father M. reminded me of the priest who baptized me. Perhaps there are still good men in the clergy, even if they are too few.

I began to attend again. Return does not erase history; it lets God rewrite its use. And I will say this plainly: I will not be silenced as a survivor of priestly abuse, and I will not bow to any mortal—collar or not. I will love the church and tell the truth about her failures. I will work for a church that guards the little ones first.

What will this look like in practice? Simple things, repeated. Scripture opened daily—not as ammunition but as bread. Prayer that is honest, even when it is only a groan. Fellowship with believers who will correct me when I wander and carry me when I am weak. Work that blesses ordinary people: the single mother counting pennies, the older man who lost his trade when the pits closed, the teenager who thinks there is no future here. I want a church that does not talk about the poor from a safe distance, but sits at their tables and lets them sit at ours. "Happy are those who consider the poor; the LORD delivers them in the day of trouble" (Ps 41:1). "Not by might, nor by power, but by my spirit, says the LORD of hosts" (Zech 4:6).

I also know my lane. I am not a militant. My calling is to teach and to tend—to help people shoulder the cross and discover that Christ is already under its weight with them. I want to speak to those who were wounded by religion and to those who were

Looking Forward

flattered by it, because both need the same Jesus. If God grants me strength, I will keep writing—poems, prayers, sayings that point away from me and toward him. Words can be a cup of cold water when they are soaked in truth.

Threads of Destiny

THERE IS ONE MORE thing I must say plainly. When I was a child, the priest who baptized me told my father that I had a calling. For years I folded that word into the corners of life like a secret map. As I have grown, the map refuses to stay hidden. I do not yet know what name this calling will wear—teacher, companion, healer, or something the church has not yet named. I only know the charge I have been given: heal with the grace that healed me, and do not let titles or safety fence you in. My path must run inside the household of faith and beyond its safest rooms, wherever my brothers and sisters are suffocating.

I will be honest: I am afraid. There are nights I weep; there are moments in a pulpit when old scenes flash and my hands tremble. The wolves of the past still scent my wounds. Yet in those same nights I feel a warm hand on my shoulder, and I hear a Father say, "I am with you." He does not promise an easy path; he promises his presence along it. And he has taught me this: when the wolves come, do not become what harmed you. Turn the other cheek—not as surrender but as a refusal to answer violence with violence. Let God judge. Keep your heart clean. Keep offering what you were given.

So I step into the next chapter—evangelical colors for the word, ancient rhythms for prayer, radical grace to guide my steps. I do not know every turn ahead, but I know who walks it. And if these pages do anything, let them be a lantern for your feet until the morning comes. "The night is far gone, the day is near" (Rom 13:12).

Bridge I—Interlude: Legacy

Silence at the font—
Jesus whispers: You are Mine;
courage drowns out fear.

Remember: Grace isn't soft escape; it's strength that stays—Christ kneeling to bind what bleeds.

Ruach in the nave—
candles find the holy sway;
faith bows—Christ holds fast.

Remember: Truth is righteous when it heals what it exposes—truth told in love.

Part II: Prophetic Psalms

NO VEIL CAN HIDE

Inspired by: Isa 5:20, Matt 23, John 8:32, Luke 18:13–14, Mic 6:8, Rom 12:19, Heb 4:13

I

You dressed your sentences in linen,
polished truth for public sight;
but cries were buried out of frame—
the altar gleamed, the heart took flight.
"Woe," sang prophets, "to sugar-tongues
that trade a wound for golden calm."
Truth is not merchandise for peace;
it burns and frees—it is a psalm.
Before Adonai all things lie open—
no mask can stand, no secret stays.
"Know truth," says Jesus—chains remember,
and leave their rattles in the grave.

II

You stacked your walls with brittle creed,
and prayed for those you would not see;
but love is more than fear's design—
it cages none, it sets us free.
The sinner, hand upon his breast,
whispers, "Be merciful to me."
Christ comes without a contract's weight,
and lifts the lowly to His seat.
Not proof, but honesty He seeks—
a humbled heart, a contrite plea;
there ḥesed stitches fractured places,
and pride makes room for saving grace.

Part II: Prophetic Psalms

III

Tremble not—leave wrath to God;
the Judge is just, His timing wise.
Do justice; love mercy; walk humbly,
beneath His wide and open skies.
Nothing hides from holy eyes;
the trees will show the seeds we sow.
Where Ruach falls like quiet rain,
new mercies root and righteousness grows.
No hand can hold what God makes whole;
no veil can dim His searching light.
O Lord, make true our inward parts,
and set our steps in shalom's life. Amen.

NO SWORD, NO WALL

Inspired by: Matt 26:52, Isa 2:4, Luke 22:51, Mic 6:8, Rom 12:18-21, Eph 2:13-22, John 18:36

I

Hands rose high in painted light
while Mercy wept outside the frame.
Pulpits thundered law and grace—
the deeper silence kept its blame.
On midnight ground the Lamb bent low;
Gethsemane still knows His name.
He touched the wound our zeal had cut,
and spoke His peace into our shame:
"Put back your blade," the Savior says—
our borrowed fire goes out, revealed;
in His good scars our pride is tried,
our war-born righteousness unsealed.

II

They sang of peace with martial chords,
of kingdoms forged by iron right;
but Truth walks barefoot through the ash
and will not kneel to blood or might.
"My kingdom is not from this world,"
the Holy One of Calvary calls.
He is our Peace; in His own flesh
He broke hostilities and walls.
No steel can draw the Way of Christ;
His shalom is mercy's reign—
where enemies learn common bread,
and grace unthreads the ancient chain.

Part II: Prophetic Psalms

III

So set down myths that crown our fear,
the tremor hiding under rage.
He will not march beneath our flags,
nor bless our dread with sacred page.
Beat swords to ploughshares; let love face
the justice ḥesed dares to name.
As far as it depends on you,
seek peace—overtake wrong with grace.
From font and table hear His call:
"Not this. Choose peace in My good Name."
O Spirit, make our courage meek—
no sword, no wall—just Gospel flame. Amen.

THE WAY IS SLAIN

Inspired by: Luke 18:9-14, John 10:7-11, Matt 23:27-28, Phil 2:5-11, Matt 7:13-14, Rom 6:5-8, Isa 53

I

Torches lifted, voices high—
yet Mercy never heard her name.
You bowed to thrones, you bought a veil;
the borrowed light went thin and tame.
White stone gleamed while graves breathed dust;
the hymn kept time, the heart kept cold.
Not bought by wealth or staged acclaim,
the Shepherd waits and calls by name:
"I am the Door," He speaks with grace—
and bruised ones cross into His rest.

II

The scroll was read, the credo said—
but soil stayed hard and justice fled.
You held the words, denied the cry;
you saw the cross and passed it by.
He asks no robe, no gilded throne,
but servants shaped to match His own—
who emptied Self and took the slave,
kenosis crowned with higher Name.
The gate is narrow, bending low;
the proud step back, the humbled go.
"Be merciful," the sinner pleads—
and ḥesed meets the deepest need.

Part II: Prophetic Psalms

III

Step from the dais, gilded seat;
Truth walks barefoot, bruised, and meek.
No mask survives refining fire;
no title stands that cannot bless.
With Christ we die; with Christ we rise—
His wounded hands our righteousness.
"The Good Shepherd lays down His life"—
and by His stripes we heal again.
The Door is Love; the Way is slain—
hope waits, scar-bright, beyond the veil.
O Ruach, breathe; make courage kind,
and send us in Jesus' Name. Amen.

GIVEN TO US

*Inspired by: Isa 1:11–17, Mic 6:6–8, Matt 21:12–14,
Luke 4:18–19, Acts 7:48–50, Eph 2:8–9, Rom 8:15*

I

They lifted towers—cold with law—
and ringed the heart with edicts tight.
But Love had planted deeper seed
beneath the streets, beneath the might.
Steel forgets; the thrones grow dim—
their borrowed glory burns to dusk.
What hammers frame with rule and flame
can never hold the Holy Trust.
Adonai will not be housed;
no stone can roof unmeasured grace.
The Lord of heaven walks our dust,
and meets the poor in open space.

II

No coin can purchase breath or light;
no ledger cages what You are.
They sold our fear for profit's gain—
grace broke the lock and walked the bar.
By gift—not wage—we stand made free,
saved by Your mercy, not our claim;
no longer slaves to dread or shame,
but children crying, "Abba—Name!"
The Christ who swept the courts of trade
now heals the lame and calls the lost;
good news for poor, release for bound—
Your ḥesed flows from cross to cross.

Part II: Prophetic Psalms

III

So let the empires ash and fade;
let idols fracture, systems fall.
The Gift remains—unbought, unearned—
a lamp that out-sings midnight's call.
O Spirit—Ruach—stir our bones;
bear witness we are Yours by grace.
Then justice, mercy, humble walk
become the anthem of our days.
Given, not earned—our birthright fire:
in Jesus' Name we rise and praise;
from font and table, sent in love,
to widen shalom's open ways. Amen.

CHRIST WEPT ONCE MORE

Inspired by: Eph 2:14-16, Gal 3:28, Rev 7:9, Isa 58:6-10, Amos 5:21-24, Matt 23:23, Jas 2:1-9

I

You knelt beneath the steeple's glow
yet kept your love behind a gate.
You preached the blood and starved the bond—
you named the King and nursed the hate.
The pews were bright, the windows high;
while mercy waited at the door.
He Himself is our Peace—and still
He walked our aisles and wept once more.
O Christ, anoint our hearts with ḥesed—
let love weigh more than form and show.

II

You sang of grace and stacked up walls,
etched creed on stone with sharpened edge;
you crowned your symbols, hushed the poor,
and bent the pulpit to a ledge.
But Truth will not be gagged or sold—
the weightier matters still demand:
do justice, mercy, faithfulness;
no partial palms at grace's hand.
Our Peace has torn the hostile veil—
let enmity be laid to rest.

Part II: Prophetic Psalms

III

His blood is not a private stream—
no border hems the gift He gave.
From every tribe He stitches one Body:
one cross, one table, one shared grave.
Loose every yoke; unclench the claim;
let fasting turn to bread and light.
O Ruach, meet us where we yield—
make brave our love; make wrong things right.
In Christ there's neither slave nor free—
one new humanity made whole.
Turn now and walk in humble shalom;
the Day draws near. Amen.

THE TRUE KING

Inspired by: Zech 9:9, Luke 4:18-19, Matt 25:31-46, Phil 2:6-11, Rev 19:11-16, Isa 1:17, Mic 6:8

I

They bowed to suits and silver tongues
and missed the scars in open palms.
Altars gleamed; the alleys wept;
their psalms grew bright while justice waned.
No throne can house the Nazarene—
He walks where ḥesed braves the street.
"Behold, your King"—a humble colt;
He chooses dust for royal seat.
Where power poses, Mercy moves;
the true procession passes low.

II

They quoted law with lifted hands,
then shut the doors and drew the sword;
they tailored peace to fit command,
and bent the pulpit toward a lord.
But Christ is not a nation's pawn,
nor stitched to empire's heavy thread:
He feeds the poor, He frees the bound;
His first throne stood among the dead.
He emptied self, took servant form—
to Him each knee will learn to bend.

Part II: Prophetic Psalms

III

So crown Him not with golden lies,
nor cast His Name in empire's mold.
He rules where tyrants lose their grip,
where widows eat and truth is told.
From font and table learn His way—
no seal or sword, but courage, grace.
O Lamb once slain, our Peace, our King,
send us to seek the orphan's case:
do right; love mercy; humbly walk—
Your kingdom comes as servants serve. Amen.

I FORGIVE YOU, BROTHER

Inspired by: Rom 8:1–2, Gal 3:28, John 13:34–35, 2 Pet 3:15–16, Acts 9:1–6, 1 Cor 13

I

You wrote like fire they handled cold—
words meant to free, worn hard as mail.
They fenced the door with borrowed lines
and missed the mercy in the veil.
Some letters, Peter said, run deep—
and twisted, make the weary small;
the loads grew heavy, love grew thin,
and fear sat high in sacred halls.
Yet through the page Christ still declares:
"No condemnation—rise from there."

II

I see the man behind the ink—
the road, the light, the sudden fall;
the scales, the thorn, the borrowed chains,
a widening table set for all.
You met the Lord and did not run;
you crossed the borders you had drawn—
to eat with those once named "outside,"
to write love's grammar into dawn.
Not Christ Himself—yet pointing true,
you taught the Church to hope and bear.
Some words cut sharp and left me sore;
and others healed me to the core.

Part II: Prophetic Psalms

III

I will not say it never hurt;
but grace begins where graves have been.
In Jesus' Name I rise again—
no chains remain for those in Him.
One Body now, in Christ made one—
no slave, no free; no "us" or "them."
Let love—the better way—be known:
the mark by which we're seen as His.
So here's my yes, my living prayer:
to walk in ḥesed, hand in hand.
I choose the way of love, and say—
I forgive you, brother. Meet me at the table. Amen.

Bridge II—Interlude: Awakening

    Morning gathers us—
psalms lift like birds from shadow;
    Christ keeps the hush whole.

Remember: Justice is repair, not rhetoric—returning what was taken, doing right with ḥesed.

    Alleluia—
winter loosens grave-deep fear;
    Christ calls graves to dawn.

Remember: Peace isn't stored swords; it hammers blades to ploughshares and blesses enemies.

Part III: Creation and Kinship

Part III: Creation and Kinship

CREATION GROANS

*Inspired by: Rom 8:19–23, Gen 1:26–31, Gen 2:15, Ps 24:1,
Isa 65:17, Rev 21:1–5, Matt 6:10*

I

The earth once sown for rest and joy
now wears the bruise of grasping hands.
Hills hold their breath; old forests lean;
rivers strain beneath our plans.
Yet under fractured, fevered skies
a trembling waits—hope takes to wing:
firstfruits of the Spirit rise,
and all creation aches to sing.
Not vengeance, Lord, but childlike dawn:
show forth Your daughters, sons in Christ—
the shalom our tired fields have missed.

II

O Maker, turn our hands from waste;
unteach the hungers we have praised.
Let power open—not to seize
but mend what haste and fear have flayed.
Give courage, Jesus; grant us grace
to till and keep the dust You trust—
to guard, not gut, Your gardened world;
the earth is Yours, and we are dust.
Train hearts to seek Your kingdom come,
to do Your will with gentle might;
make stewardship a humble hymn
that honors You, O Lord of life.

Part III: Creation and Kinship

III

All creation strains toward birth—
a hymn we would not stop to hear;
yet in the dark the Spirit prays,
and living waters reappear.
"Behold, I'm making all things new"—
let that Word heal a wounded world;
tears thin before the Lamb who reigns,
till hope becomes the meadow's chord.
Lord of green and grave and grace,
send us from font and table now:
recreate our hands and days,
that earth may feel Your Kingdom's vow,
and fields at last, in You, find rest. Amen.

GREENING

Inspired by: Gen 2:15, Isa 11:6–9, Mic 4:1–4, Rom 8:19–23, Rev 21:1–5, John 3:3–8

I

They etch their borders, crown their names—
yet dust still clings to pilgrim feet.
The stars outlast our flags and laws;
the earth keeps Sabbath's older beat.
Into our hands You lay fire and seed:
to tend and keep—not clutch and own.
Creation leans toward unveiling;
Your children step into the Son.
Firstfruits of Spirit green the furrows;
the Second Adam breathes us new.
Where we have burned, Your mercy rains;
the soil remembers how to sing.

II

God of sap and stream and stone—
of snowfall hush and prairie fire—
forgive the engines we have blessed,
the hungers we mistook for choir.
Teach keeping deeper than control;
melt swords to pruning hooks again.
Let wolf lie easy with the lamb;
let fear yield to ḥesed's reign.
O Ruach, pass over dust once more;
make meek our strength, make strong our care—
and in the wounds we cut in earth
plant Christ the Wounded Healer there.

Part III: Creation and Kinship

III

So let the greening come at last—
not seized by will, but born of grace.
Let justice spring like water clear;
let mercy flower in every place.
No greater kingdom will we seek
than this: creation healed and whole.
"Behold, I'm making all things new"—
the Word that roots the world's true goal.
From font and furrow, Spirit, lead;
in Jesus' Name align our days—
renew the ground beneath our feet,
rebirth our hearts in shalom. Amen.

DECONSTRUCTION OF THE RAINBOW

Inspired by: Gen 9:12–17, Mic 6:8, Rom 1:25, John 13:35, 2 Cor 3:17

I

They lifted neon into sky
and priced the bow for passing gain;
but cloud-set arc was never trend—
it's covenant through storm and flame.
Not made for idols—tamed or sold—
we praise not sign, but Sign-Giver.
For beast and bird and humankind
Your berit stands—faithful forever.
Let hearts not trade the Craft for craft,
nor worship work of human hands;
Your ḥesed spans the swollen flood—
keep us near You, the One who stands.

II

I did not dance beneath the strobes;
I stood in open, rain-washed air—
a quieter soul, a gentler grace,
not loud, not lost, but truly there.
Teach me the justice You delight,
the humble road Your prophets frame;
let love be how Your people're known—
by how we speak each person's name.
When symbols fray and slogans tire,
let Ruach free us where You move;
for where the Spirit of the Lord is,
we breathe the liberty You choose.

Part III: Creation and Kinship

III

O God who bent Your bow through storm,
remind us what You meant to show—
not clique or conquest, party line,
but promise bright with heaven's glow.
Turn brand to blessing, sign to song;
re-school our hope to trust Your Word.
Let rainbow mean what You declared—
a mercy none must strive to earn.
Now send us: love, do justice, kindness;
walk humbly in Your steady light—
till every home finds safe repose
beneath Your covenant of life. Amen.

WILD FOLKS OF GOD

Inspired by: Job 38-41, Gen 1:24-25, Isa 11:6-9, Rom 8:19-22, Rev 5:13

I

They do not bargain with the sky
or clamor for a crown or name.
They live as given—breath and bone—
no pose to keep, no freight of shame.
"And God saw good" still hums in them;
no ox has lied, no sparrow schemed.
They never reached for stolen fruit—
no rescue pled, no boast redeemed—
just creature-courage, quiet grace.

II

The lion sleeps beneath His gaze,
untroubled by what can't be known;
the whale makes hymn of pressured depths
and calls the far blue trenches home.
He spoke them forth from formless dark,
and still He knows each fin and wing;
He calls them holy—not for proofs,
but for the goodness of their being.
What ḥesed fashioned, they abide.

Part III: Creation and Kinship

III

O dust-born children, quick to stray,
we chase the light and lose the road;
while hind and hawk keep hymn and hush
and walk their praise where grasses bode.
Creation waits for sons revealed—
for daughters standing in the Son;
till wolf and lamb lie down in peace
and every creature, sea and sun,
cries, "Worthy is the Lamb who reigns!"
Teach us that wild, faithful art:
be made anew in Christ alone—
and praise with glad, unguarded heart. Amen.

MORE THAN A DOG

Inspired by: Prov 12:10, Matt 6:26, Job 12:7–10, Isa 11:6–9, Rom 8:19–22

I

You came with wounds the world miscounted—
a winter-breath beneath the snow;
yet in your gaze a mercy burned
more fierce than many pulpits know.
"Ask of the beasts," the Scripture says—
and there I learned a gentler art:
He numbers sparrows as they fall,
and Christ kept watch on both our hearts.
Your tremble found my hidden dread;
Love widened room, and ḥesed spread.

II

Your legs were iron, yet your will ran free—
a limping hymn that reached for me.
No creed, no speech—just breath and dust;
still faith was schooled in patient trust.
The righteous learn a creature's life,
through frost and heat, through storm and strife;
and under Ruach's quiet lead
my grip uncurled to humble heed.
Each wait, each howl, each fragile hour
became the fire that gentled power.

Part III: Creation and Kinship

III

They say no soul can wear your shape—
yet veils grow thin where mercies wake.
If wolves make peace and fields are healed,
and groaning earth is set to sing,
then let the Shepherd—Lord of all—
hold every living, trembling thing.
Beneath His wings we rest and rise;
He mends what sorrow's night has torn.
Till all creation learns shalom,
run where the lilies greet the morn—
and where His Mercy opens space,
we'll meet in Christ's bright dawn. Amen.

THREE MOTHERS

Inspired by: Ruth 1:16, Prov 31:26, Isa 49:15, Matt 12:48–50, Luke 8:21, Rom 16:13, John 19:26–27

I

When they said mother, I turned my face—
the word was heavy, near the wound.
Those who bore me brought no balm;
their "holy fear" still taught me fear.
They named me wrong before I spoke;
the blessing bent, the lesson broke.
Yet even if a mother leaves,
You do not loose Your grip, O Lord.
"I will not forget," You said—
my name is etched upon Your palms.
You held my breath, You kept my heart,
and made me brave with quiet peace.

II

Then three arose in smaller rooms—
no blood between, but love alight:
a teacher with the torah of kindness,
a coach who would not quit the fight,
a coder's patient, steady hands
repairing what the others broke.
Where you go, I go—Ruth on their lips;
and at the door, Rome's greeting rang:
"Be mother to me—mine as well."
I chose them back with ḥesed strong;
and hope relearned its mother-tongue.

Part III: Creation and Kinship

III

No marble saints, no chrismed robes—
just Christ within their open hands.
From Calvary still comes the charge:
"Behold your mother"—family made.
"For those who do My Father's will
are brother, sister, mother named."
So gather us to one wide table;
let first the mercies enter in—
the ones who mothered where love lacked.
O Jesus, weave this holy kin;
keep us in love that does not end. Amen.

BROTHERS OR SISTERS?

Inspired by: Gen 1:27, Luke 15:20–24, Ps 34:18, Rom 12:15, Matt 23:4, Gal 3:28

I

"Go play with brothers," voices said—
but gentler hands drew me to grace.
Their games were kind; no hidden bruise,
no lesson carved on tender face.
Yet boys were handed iron scripts:
be steel, don't feel—never be kind.
Imago Dei: I stood in light,
a tender son with open hands;
and winter's shame cut thin and cold—
but You, O Lord, did not condemn.

II

They chased the ball, they climbed the rope,
as if a quiet war were on;
I stayed with ribbons, careful joy—
and whispered names grew barbed and strong.
Now, Lord, I see the weight they bore—
the fathers' creed, the Sunday yoke
that piles its loads and starves delight.
Be near the crushed, as You have spoke;
teach us to weep with those who weep,
and loose the cords of heavy codes.

Part III: Creation and Kinship

III

What curse makes sons afraid to feel?
What creed demands we scorn the weak?
I loved them still—my fellow lambs—
all shepherded by Christ who speaks.
O Father running down the road,
O Shepherd calling each by name,
make brave our hearts with gentle grace;
let dignity for all remain.
No male nor female—one in Christ;
one table spread, one hearth, one flame.
From distant playgrounds gather us—
in ḥesed, make our household whole. Amen.

BOND REMAINS

Inspired by: Ruth 1:16-17, Rom 8:38-39, 2 Tim 1:5, Heb 12:1, 1 Cor 13:7-8, John 15:13

I

Ash on your knuckles, night for bread;
you traded silence into song.
You broke so I could learn to dream;
your quiet pain stitched hope along.
Then time collapsed—a breath, a fall—
the forest hushed, the sky drew small;
yet through the dusk your vow held true:
"Where you go, I will go too."
Love made us brave with gentle grace,
and Christ our Fellow Traveler kept pace.

II

Across the sea with work-worn palms,
you sent me warmth through wire and storm;
they bent your name, dismissed your worth—
but covenant love—ḥesed—held form.
A father's faith, a grandfather's too—
old prayers like threads that carried through;
not perfect, no, but tried and strong:
it bore, believed, hoped, endured long.
Mercy, Cross-won and running free,
lifted my life and steadied me.

Part III: Creation and Kinship

III

No crown, no stage, no marble grace—
just hands that found the holy place:
your hands, His hands—same worn design,
the Shepherd's touch that rescued mine.
With saints who are a circling cloud,
at font and grave the vow stays loud:
no height, nor depth, nor years that roll
can sever what His mercies hold.
"Greater love"—He laid life down—
and still our bond remains in Him. Amen.

Bridge III—Interlude: Exiled Child

>Rain on churchyard stone—
>names sleep; Christ keeps them by name;
>mercy keeps the watch.

Remember: Repentance is more than tears; it bears amends—fruit that fits repentance.

>Night keeps its silence—
>Spirit names the hidden ache;
>Christ steadies the dark.

Remember: Wisdom isn't knowing everything; it asks, "Lord, give wisdom," and walks humbly.

Part IV: Lament and Healing

GOOD LIKE FIRE

Inspired by: Ps 88, Lam 3, Job 38–42, Isa 6:1–7, Heb 12:29, Matt 21:12–13, Rom 8:22–28, John 11:35, Rev 1:17–18

I

Do not hand me "God is good" as if it ends the ache—
as if it fills a mother's lungs at graveside dusk,
as if prayer could not return with empty hands.
The tomb still echoes; Psalm 88 still sings.
I need the God who steps into dust and sorrow,
who weeps at Lazarus' stone and yet walks on—
who knew our frame (He wore our frame)
and breathes again into the dust.
Not slogan, but a Savior—Jesus:
mercy with scars, ḥesed that holds.

II

Where is the weight—the Voice that thundered Job to wonder?
Where is the Christ who cleared the courts
not for a point but because the air was choking?
Yes—God is good; but not like lacquered cheer,
not like a tag that sticks to pain.
He is good like coal to trembling lips,
good like consuming fire that spares the heart
and burns the lie away;
good like mercy breaking chains,
like light that drops us to our knees
before it heals our sight.
This goodness shoulders cross and dawn—
and names us free.

Part IV: Lament and Healing

III

This is more than a line; it is witness—
the ache of saints, the hush of martyrs,
the midnight tears of pastors out of words.
He is no slogan to be sold—
He is the storm survived, the temple shaken,
the Ruach groaning in our bones toward hope.
He is the First and Last: "Fear not,"
keys in hand over death and Hades.
So if we say, "God is good,"
let it be as those who've seen the grave
and met the Risen One—
who rise by grace, made brave and gentle,
to love, to serve, to trust His Name.
Good like fire; good like mercy; good like Jesus. Amen.

BLIGHTED MAN

Inspired by: Gen 1:27, Rom 8:23, John 20:27-28, Ps 139:14-16, 1 Cor 6:19-20, Isa 53:3-5

I

They named the flesh a trap, a test—
yet dawn remembers dust called good.
Imago Dei marks this frame;
it was this body wept and bled,
this body carried unanswered prayers.
Between two altars—home and school—
I starved on silence, thin with fear;
but You kept vigil in my skin
and counted bone and breath as Yours.

II

They handed candles, quiet, shame,
and promised heaven if I thinned—
spirit split from skin like rind.
But at the table: "My Body," Christ—
and chrism traced a cross on mine.
No ghost for God—the Word took flesh
and keeps it for the healing still:
by His own stripes our wounds find place;
this temple's Yours—bought, not our will.
Your Ruach breathes through breath and bone;
You dwell where others taught me hide.

Part IV: Lament and Healing

III

I walk—half-ghost, yet sacrament—
still seeking You who will not flinch.
Grant Thomas' reach to touch the wounds
and cry, "My Lord and my God," sure.
Till groaning bodies hope made whole,
and Spirit-courage steadies limbs,
You read the lines they tried to blot
and name me wondrous, feared and formed.
Still hoping. Still in skin. Still held by ḥesed.
Still Yours, O Christ. Amen.

AM I WICKED?

Inspired by: 1 Sam 16:7, Ps 139:13-16, Matt 23:4, John 8:7-11, John 10:27, Rom 8:1, Isa 43:1

I

They drew their borders round a face,
tied heavy yokes on gentle frames;
said light must dress a single way,
and softness ought to hide its name.
But I was child—alive to grace,
hands making praise in simple art.
Men looked at height and outward show;
the Lord looked in and did not start.
He knows the work His fingers formed—
fearfully made, He knows my heart.

II

So I asked Jesus—not the crowd,
not stones disguised as borrowed law—
"Am I made wrong for loving light,
for standing soft, not built for war?"
He stooped and wrote His answer low—
no stone to throw, just mercy's tone.
"My sheep will know My voice," He said;
"No condemnation—you are Mine."
He called my name with ḥesed strong;
fear loosed its knots beneath His sign.

Part IV: Lament and Healing

III

Here do I stand—still flesh and breath,
a man who longs for covenant,
drawn to what's strong yet kind and true,
not cruelty masked as confidence.
Am I wicked—or a witness
to paradox the Potter planned:
Ruach-breathed, wonderfully made,
beloved, written on His hand?
Let others clutch their borrowed wool—
I trust the Shepherd's faithful word:
"You are redeemed, called by your name;
Mine, not cast off." Amen.

THE PARENT WHO WAITS

Inspired by: Isa 64:8, Rom 8:19-22, Heb 12:7-11, Luke 15:11-20, Hab 1:2-3, Gen 1:28

I

They say a Father moves the world—
and sometimes all He does is stay:
no thunder split, no firefall,
a hush wide enough to pray.
O Potter, patient over clay—
not here to crush, but form and hold—
You keep the watch, breath-close, unnamed;
Your ḥesed tenses into open arms,
eyes on the road for children home;
and when the dust lifts—You run.

II

"How long, O Lord?" the ache repeats,
as Habakkuk once wept and pled;
creation labors, sore with hope,
its breath a tide that will not quit.
Yet into mortal hands You press
the tools to tend, to mend, to lift—
to till and keep, to steady knees,
to learn the fruit Your trainings give.
A Father does not still each storm;
He grieves, then girds with grace and courage,
and sets the work within our reach.

Part IV: Lament and Healing

III

Call not our Father far removed—
Your image lives in dust and bone.
In Christ made flesh Your mercy walked,
and by His cross brought exiles home.
O Ruach, breathe in weary lungs;
teach gentle strength, make patience art.
You wait the way good parents wait—
not wrath, but fierce believing heart:
that we will carry what You gave
and love the world You will not "fix."
Then when we turn, You run to meet—
and send us out to serve. Amen.

DID ANYONE ASK GOD?

Inspired by: Isa 1:2–4, Ps 22:1–3, Luke 22:42–44, John 1:10–11, Rom 8:26–27

I

We storm the heavens—rain, then fire—
for open doors and dreams made real.
We pile requests like stacked commands,
and miss the Giver for the gifts.
"Hear, O heavens," prophets cried;
we pray and turn our faces off.
O Holy One whose heart is kind—
did anyone ask, Are You okay?
Teach us to love the Lord of grace,
not only what His hands can give.

II

Since Eden's break You've borne our ache—
You came unto Your very own,
and doors were latched, and timber rough.
In Gethsemane: "Not Mine, but Yours"—
sweat falling red, the chalice kept.
"My God, My God"—the psalm You prayed;
the Man of Sorrows would not flee.
Let ḥesed slow our hurried feet
to keep the watch where Love once wept;
let mercy teach us how to stay.

Part IV: Lament and Healing

III

So let petitions rest a while—
no proof to stage, no easy glow;
just silence deep enough for love,
a child who lingers, hears You breathe.
When words go thin, the Ruach sighs—
groans too deep, yet clear as day;
and we grow brave with quiet grace
to whisper, "Abba . . . are You okay?"
Then rise to serve Your wounded world—
"Your will be done," in Jesus' Name. Amen.

BLACK SHEEP

Inspired by: Luke 15:4-7, Isa 53:3, Matt 23:4-5, Ps 34:18, Rom 8:38-39, John 10:14, 1 Sam 16:7

I

They stacked their books with lines in red;
shame slept, folded, in each page.
Hands held a light with winter eyes;
the polished pews shone past my ache.
I waited—small, a narrowed breath—
while judgment posed as careful care;
but near the brokenhearted One,
Love came and took the other chair.

II

They spoke my name as if it burned,
as though my breath could stain the floor;
they weighed my sins in whisper-scales,
locked kindness with a bolted door.
Yet through the seams of brittle hymns
Mercy moved and knew my name—
the Shepherd crossed their chalk-drawn lines;
in ḥesed I stood up, unashamed.

III

They chant the saints and number shame;
I keep the dust and will not bow.
"The Lord sees heart," the prophet says—
and I am known by Jesus now.
Despised, rejected—so was He;
His shoulders found me, black and thin.
No height, nor depth, nor darkest night
can pry me from His wounded hands.
I am the hymn they would not sing—
He sings it over me. Amen.

TOO MUCH LIGHT

Inspired by: Isa 42:3, John 10:27–29, Rom 8:15, Matt 23:4, Ps 34:18, 1 John 4:18

I

They mortared "grace" in granite walls;
stone goes cold when hunger calls.
They crowned the sun and named it pure—
too much light scalds, will not cure.
A child stood quiet—bruised reed, thin;
a wick that trembled in the wind—
and near the crushed the Lord drew close;
Mercy stooped and held me safe.
No trumpet wrath, no iron creed—
only Jesus, gentle with my need.

II

They dressed me up in names and fear,
with yokes that bit and burdens seared;
tongues turned to ash when sorrow spoke—
they chased a flame and breathed the smoke.
For gold can bind as tight as chain,
and silence hums the loudest shame.
Still through the cracks the Shepherd came—
not wrath, but ḥesed called my name:
"My sheep know Me—do not be seized;
perfect love dismisses fear."
The Spirit whispered, "Child, be free."
"Abba," I answered, "Abba—near."

Bridge III—Interlude: Exiled Child

III

"Let go," He said, "what you were told—
their pain is not the shape of your soul.
Break off that script; those lines were wrong—
My truth in you is fierce and strong.
Not theirs to bind, not theirs to claim;
your life is sealed within My Name.
Be brave with grace—bear who you are;
no thief can reach My wounded scars.
I hold you fast—now rise and stand;
none shall snatch you from My hand."
Held there, my heart learns quiet light—shalom. Amen.

Bridge IV—Interlude: Paschal Hope

Ash upon our brows—
Ruach shields the tender flame;
Jesus tends it bright.

Remember: Duty is holy in the unseen—kept at first light where only the Father sees.

Paschal light now spent—
wax rivers hymn the timber;
Christ outshines the night.

Remember: Strength is proved by sheathing steel—choosing shalom over thunder.

Part V: Contemplative Pieces

BEAUTY OF HOLINESS

Inspired by: Gen 1:1–3; Gen 2:7; John 1:1–5, 14; Exod 19;
Luke 2:7; Jas 2:13; 2 Cor 3:3

I

Before the clocks, a hush—Your Breath hovering.
Not only temples know the fire; dust remembers Your hands.
Stone keeps the rumor of Your Name; clay keeps the kiss.
Light said Be, and the dark learned a new grammar.
You, Word become flesh, walked into our dusk with a lamp.
Holiness came as heat and kindness—
a flame that knows our names, a hand that does not withdraw.
Creation answered like a choir finding pitch:
beauty becoming prayer, prayer becoming light.
Light and peace in Your Name.

II

The weaver prays in thread; the painter baptizes color.
Dancers spell the psalms with ankles and air.
All art under the cross is wound turned gold—
Sinai thunders truth; Bethlehem hushes mercy close.
The Word-made-flesh keeps moving in ordinary rhythm:
water, bread, neighbor—font, table, doorbell.
Each gift mirrors the Giver; every breath returns as thanks.
Rubble, surrendered, learns cathedral;
for the Lamb's verdict is mercy over judgment.
Here, courage studies the syntax of grace,
and heaven leans low to listen.

Part V: Contemplative Pieces

III

Spirit—Ruach—hover again;
write not on stone, but on us: living letters.
Breathe through brushstroke, cadence, refrain;
make our small hands vessels for Your brightness.
Take the forgotten things—make them altar.
Lead us by Passover to the Table,
through wilderness to living water,
to the Vine where branches learn to sing.
Give us light to bear, and gentleness to bear it.
Send us to love and serve in Jesus' Name,
till errands become psalms
and every soul turns gallery of light.
Not performance but Presence: Adonai-with-us.
This is the beauty of holiness. Amen.

SPRING OF LIFE

Inspired by: John 4:10-14, Isa 55:1-3, Matt 11:28-30, Rev 22:1-2, Rom 8:26, Ps 23:2, Ezek 47:9

I

Not on hammered gold, nor in thunder's borrowed pride—
but where roots drink quiet light and silence breathes: the Deep abides.
No fist of wrath, no scorching name; only the clear, unhurrying river—
crystal peace, a hush beneath the world's loud claim.
At Jacob's well, at noonday heat, He waits and speaks our names;
He asks for water and gives a spring.
Word-made-flesh, You meet the storm-worn,
give courage, grant us grace—and stay.
Where earthly power fractures and fails,
Your gentleness outlasts the noise;
Your life sings in the throat of the well,
and thirst becomes a door.

II

"Come, all who thirst"—the price is thirst.
No coin, no measured deed.
Not distant on steepled heights,
You meet us where we truly need.
Wide water, sheer gift; the Tree blooms under ash,
its leaves learning the nations back to health.
Ruach within us, sighing depths no tongue can carry—
groans that braid with hope.
Living water rises slow, steady as dawn,
till heads are lifted and hearts made strong.
Wherever this river moves, dead places quicken;
the desert finds a choir;
banks grow green with mercy's sound.

Part V: Contemplative Pieces

III

Not debt, nor dread, nor iron vow—
but rest and rhythm, holy time.
"Come to Me"; Your yoke is kind,
Your burden light—a Sabbath sign.
You lead us by the quiet streams;
Your ḥesed names us known and loved.
So drink, my soul, the living light;
receive the hush no fear can own.
O Spring who sings beneath the soil,
make brave our hearts with gentle grace;
then send us out—from font and table—
to bless the world You mean to raise,
till every street bears shalom's sound
and all creation rises. Amen.

DEAR LOVE

Inspired by: John 20:1-18, Rom 5:8, Isa 53:5, Col 2:13-14, 1 John 4:7-12, Rom 12:9-16, Matt 22:37-40

I

Before the horn, before the sun,
the garden learned a new word: Rise.
The stone forgot its duty;
silence remembered our names.
Not wrath displayed but ḥesed shown—
Love chose the fire and wore our scars;
the Wounded One made wounds a door,
and walked the prisoners past their bars.
Our record—ink gone to mercy—nailed and cancelled;
the Crucified stands as Friend.
Alleluia—Jesus lives;
morning tastes like forgiven breath.

II

So rise—not with parade, but steady mercy.
The Risen One lends courage to our ribs;
His Spirit fills the waiting space.
The blood that cleanses does not curse;
the cross that judges also frees.
At font and table, roots take hold;
hope stands tall like living trees.
Where fear once wrote the final line,
the empty tomb becomes the rhyme;
time keeps Paschal measure now—
a cadence drawing wanderers home.

Part V: Contemplative Pieces

III

O Love beyond all loves we name,
teach us to prize Your worth aright:
to hold each other, scarred and real,
as vessels warmed by Paschal light.
Let love be genuine and clean;
let honor lead and courage bow.
You call the low, the loud, the faint—
one Body learning Christ for now.
Great Love who loved us first and most,
Your law remains our highest call:
to love our God with heart and mind,
and love our neighbor—one and all.
Send us to serve in Jesus' Name,
till every road bears shalom's release. Amen.

MORNING WATCH

Inspired by: Ps 130:5–6, Lam 3:22–24, Rom 8:26, Isa 40:29–31, Matt 28:19, Acts 2:1–4, Ps 139

I

No brass, no burdened summons—only breath and holy hush.
We keep the watch; the Watcher keeps us.
Night forgets its argument under ḥesed;
mercies rise like bread of light.
O Jesus, rise within our breathing;
tune our lips to truthful praise.
Teach our hearts the first psalm of the day—
"Great is Your faithfulness"—and still the dark.
Your dawn unthreads the fear from morning;
hope stands, warm as new air.

II

O Sovereign Flame, O Silent King,
strengthen the thin places; reweave the frayed.
Let weariness bow—not to defeat—
but to the weight of mercy.
Ruach, come as wind and fire;
baptize this dawn in the Threefold Name—
Father, Son, and Holy Ghost.
Make the timid brave for good news:
at font and table, Christ is near and reigns.
Let courage find its tongue;
let peace take up its place among us.

Part V: Contemplative Pieces

III

Threefold Mystery—Breath and Flame—
the world turns slow beneath Your gaze.
You search and know us, Adonai;
each step is held, each shadow weighed.
We hurry neither naming You
nor forging songs to prove You near.
We simply wait while Deep calls Deep—
the Spirit sighing what we cannot say—
till hope takes wing; and those who trust
run, walk, and rise in quiet shalom. Amen.

SUMMER HAS COME

Inspired by: Song 2:11–13, Rom 8:11, Acts 2:1–4, Matt 6:28–30, Ps 118:24, Eccl 3:11, Gal 5:22–23

I

Gray breaks—light cleaves the sky;
the world leans gladly toward the flame.
What silence froze begins to sing—
no longer numb, no longer tame.
Ruach moves through branches green,
Pentecost in leaf and bloom.
"The winter's past," the Bridegroom calls;
hope makes space and grants it room.
Alleluia.

II

O God of warmth and rising days,
You write in light across our skies.
Your children dance beneath the sun,
released from asking how or why.
"Consider lilies"—kept by care—
each step a psalm, each laugh a seed.
From font and table, joy runs free;
Your ḥesed widens every need,
and courage grows in gentle peace.

Part V: Contemplative Pieces

III

And we—like buds that do not last—
are held within Your faithful hand.
Still You plant and still You tend
with rain and love and kind command.
The Spirit who raised Christ from death
now quickens root and bone and breath,
till fruit matures through storm and strife—
love, joy, peace; a patient heart;
kindness, goodness; faithful life;
then gentleness and self-control.
"This is the day the Lord has made"—
send us to serve in quiet grace.
Summer sings: we still belong.
The Light has come; we live by grace. Amen.

HARVEST

Inspired by: Gen 1:28–31, Ps 104, Col 3:23, Prov 14:23, Matt 25:35–40, Amos 5:24, Isa 58:10–12, John 6:12

I

Praise rises from more than fields—
from tide and kiln, from forge and flame.
From furrow, circuit, loom, and lathe,
each craft still whispers out Your Name.
Lord of the harvest, bless our toil—
the calloused hand, the sleepless light.
We work unto the Lord in Christ,
and find our labor bathed in light.
What grace—what ḥesed—fills our days:
make brave our work; receive our praise.

II

O Spirit—Ruach—through the mine,
the humming line, the city's bones:
be near the ones we seldom see,
whose hidden strength upholds our homes.
For yields we gathered yet not sown,
for unseen tables, debts we owe—
"the least of these": we meet You there;
to serve our neighbor is to know
the Bread of Life who breaks and gives,
then says, "Gather what remains,"
that nothing lost be left behind—
let mercy bind our scattered grains.
Make us repairers of the breach;
let generous justice be our speech.

Part V: Contemplative Pieces

III

Praise the Maker of the machine,
of tempered steel and patient code;
praise hands that heal, minds quick to mend,
and hearts that lift a brother's load.
Let righteousness like waters roll,
let justice stream through every street;
let fasting loose the cords of wrong,
till hungry ones have bread to eat.
"Gather the fragments," Lord of Life—
send us from font and table now,
to love and serve in Jesus' Name,
till earth made new becomes our home,
and every household knows shalom. Amen.

SPARK TO FLAME

Inspired by: Isa 42:1-3, Luke 4:18-19, Matt 25:35-40,
Jas 2:15-17, Mic 6:8, 1 Kgs 19:11-13, Rom 12:11, Ezek 36:26

I

Lamp for the worn, hush for the frayed—
a prayer on dry lips, thin but real.
The world still groans in rusted chains;
old stains speak loud, old sorrows kneel.
You stand where sutures will not hold—
not crowned by force but crowned by tears:
the Servant who will not break the bruised,
who guards the wick through wind and years.
In Nazareth You read our names—
"Ruach Adonai is upon Me."
From grief You coax a living coal;
mercy leans close and breathes it free—
an ember kept through storm and war,
to make us brave with gentle grace.

II

Shelter the broken; lift the least.
Feed with bread and make for peace.
Let city gates unlock, not sort;
let justice walk, not stall in court.
Friend of the cast-out, Lord of the dry,
You move through famine, fear, and sky.
For faith that will not work is dead—
do justice; love ḥesed; walk humbly, led.
We find You with "the least of these";
to serve is sight, to touch is know.
Where pride runs cold and hearts go hard,
Your Cross rekindles holy glow.

Part V: Contemplative Pieces

III

O breathe again, O Ruach mild—
not in the quake or blazing storm,
but in the whisper of our names,
the quiet that remakes our form.
Take away stone—give flesh instead;
write mercy where our fear once bled.
Make fervent spirits, quick to serve—
zeal for the Risen One we love.
Let forests heal and oceans mend;
teach open hands to break and share.
Till justice dawns in running light
and nations walk by Gospel care—
turn every spark to holy flame,
and send us out in Jesus' Name. Amen.

PRAY FOR A WORLD

Inspired by: Matt 19:14, Isa 42:2-3, Song 8:6, 1 Cor 13:4-7, Rom 12:9-18, Mic 6:8, Luke 6:36

I

Pray for the child who answers to Silence,
whose shelter hangs on borrowed breath.
"Let the little ones come to Me," says Jesus—
Love that outlives even death.
He will not snap the bruised nor quench the small;
teach homes to heal, not test or tease—
a welcome given without a price,
a room where fear unlearns its knees.
Let every "no" be holy guard,
and every "yes" be gentle peace;
make brave our love with quiet strength,
and mark our dread with shalom's release.

II

Redeem desire from the old shame;
by ḥesed, keep our bodies whole.
Let love be patient, kind, and true—
a vow that frees and tends the soul.
Set seals upon each faithful heart—
love strong as death, a holy flame;
a covenant both fierce and kind,
not bent by fear nor built for gain.
Teach honest yes and honest no;
let touch be blessing, never debt.
In Christ—whose cross has named us Yours—
teach us to cherish what You've set.

Part V: Contemplative Pieces

III

Pray for the ones who stand exposed,
whose voices crack and still they speak.
Let nations serve the least as first;
teach rulers how to carry meek.
Let love be real—unhypocrite;
outdo in honor; cleave to good.
Do justice, mercy; humbly walk;
be merciful as You have stood.
As far as it can rest with us,
let reconciled roads be our way.
Then send us out in Jesus' Name
to guard the dignity of all—
till rivers learn the shape of grace
and every house keeps Love for law. Amen.

Bridge V—Interlude: Communion

Table set with light—
Christ mends the distance as one;
cups reply: shalom.

Remember: Leadership isn't winning the room; it's setting a table for the least—"Feed My lambs."

After the sirens—
neighbors pour shalom in cups;
Your kingdom, O Christ.

Remember: Holiness doesn't stop at the altar; it carries bread beyond the door to the neighbor.

Coda: The Last Bloom

EVERY BOOK MUST END, yet the word of God does not. What you have read in these pages are not conclusions but glimpses—small, pale blooms on a greater branch. They are not answers to every ache but fragments of light that keep us walking, praying, and loving in the dark. "The grass withers, the flower fades; but the word of our God will stand forever" (Isa 40:8).

When I first began writing these pieces, I thought of them as poems. But the longer I lived with them, the more I saw they are prayers too—sometimes whispered, sometimes steady as bread in trembling hands. They are not performances. They are traces of a Presence already among us—Christ with us, Christ for us, Christ in us.

I believe with all my heart that the church still has a witness to bear in this age. Not the witness of grandeur, or of power, or of polished certainty, but the witness of mercy that binds wounds; of courage that bends but does not break; of holiness that walks beyond its doors into the world God loves. These writings are my small attempt at that witness. "By this everyone will know that you are my disciples, if you have love for one another" (John 13:35).

The title, *Pale Bloom*, is a reminder. A bloom is fragile, and a pale bloom even more so. Yet it is enough. One bloom in a field tells us spring is near. One blossom at the edge of frost shows us that death will not have the final word. One pale bloom can be overlooked—but gathered with others, it becomes a garden.

If you want companions after this book, start with Teresa of Ávila—the friend who makes prayer honest and doable. Read

Coda: The Last Bloom

The Way of Perfection when you're tired, then *Interior Castle* when you're ready to go deeper. Let Francis of Assisi loosen your grip on fear and teach joy that costs something—try *Little Flowers* for his contagious gladness, then his *Admonitions* for the sharp edge of love. And when the world feels used up, turn to Hildegard of Bingen for greening hope—*Scivias* to remember the story you live in, *Symphonia* to let your prayer sing. Teresa makes prayer real, Francis makes love brave, Hildegard makes hope green—perfect next steps when you turn this last page.

All three point to one thread: radical grace. By "radical grace," I mean the mercy of Jesus that names sin truthfully and then stays to bind the wound. It is Christ kneeling to trace a new future in dust while stones grow quiet; Christ running down the road with robe and ring while shame rehearses its speech; Christ shouldering thorn and wood for friends who denied him; Christ the Shepherd in weather and thorns for one lost lamb—again and again. Radical grace is not a shrug; it is surgery. It does not flatter our wounds or fear our darkness; it brings light and goes with us into the long recovery. If these pages have taught anything, I pray it is this: God comes close, and his nearness is both truth and tenderness.

I have railed and I have returned. That is the shape of my love. Lovers argue because they still hope. I will not sanctify failure, nor will I call the Bride a corpse. She sometimes sleeps; she must be woken, washed, and fed. My vow is simple: I will stay and speak—for the little ones, for the bruised, for the hungry, for the ones who think they no longer belong. Real reform is born inside the house—at the table where we break the same bread.

I want doors that creak from being opened, a parish that smells like soup and incense, elders who have learned the quiet art of listening, priests who can say, "I am sorry," and a choir that includes the off-key because heaven does too. I want pulpits that thunder against abuse and hands that hold the hurting with gentleness. Teach children that holiness is not a performance but a courage; teach adults that repentance is not a collapse but a doorway. Let churches be houses where strangers become neighbors and neighbors become kin.

Part V: Contemplative Pieces

To priests, pastors, and elders: Please be brave. Do not confuse secrecy with prudence or optics with truth. If you must choose between protecting an image and protecting a child, let the image burn. The gospel can stand the fire; reputations cannot save. Let your hearts burn instead—with love for the small, with grief for our failures, with a hunger for righteousness that is more than a word in a creed. When you have done right, do not trumpet it; wash your hands, weep if you must, and ask how to do better still. You were not ordained to defend systems but to tend souls. "What does the LORD require of you but to do justice, and to love kindness, and to walk humbly with your God?" (Mic 6:8).

To the wounded: You are not what was done to you. You are not what you did. You are a person in whom God delights. He says your name with a smile, even when you do not. If you cannot believe this yet, borrow my belief until yours returns. If you cannot pray, breathe; if you cannot breathe, sit; if you cannot sit, let someone sit with you. The Spirit prays when you cannot. The church is meant to kneel when you cannot. If the church will not, then call me, and I will.

I have stood on the shoreline and wanted the horizon more than the hull. But the One who rules the sea sleeps in this boat. Wake him with your fear. He is not offended by weather; he speaks to it. He will rebuke the wind and our despair—not to shame us but to give us back the sky. Faith is not never being afraid; it is remembering who is in the boat and where his word sends us.

In the beginning, God planted a garden and walked in the cool of the day. At the end, a city descends like a bride, and at its heart is a river, and on either side trees whose leaves heal nations. Between garden and garden we live among briars, yet we are asked to tend and to keep, to sow and to sing. A pale bloom in a crack of concrete is not sentiment; it is a sign—an early leaf from the trees to come, a small announcement that the future has already started. Bow to it. Tend to it. Join it.

And so I leave you with this: "Now may the Lord of peace himself give you peace at all times in all ways. The Lord be with all of you" (2 Thess 3:16). May that peace make you brave, and may

Coda: The Last Bloom

every pale bloom you meet—on a windowsill, at a graveside, in a sanctuary, on a sidewalk—remind you that the Word still walks our fields and will not let the last word be winter.

Appendix:
Guardrails / Mental Health Helplines

GUARDRAILS

These are guardrails, not gimmicks—habits that keep me near Christ and the church.

1. Scripture first. Every impression bows to the word already given. If there's tension, Scripture wins.
2. Community counsel. I test experiences with pastors, elders, and trauma-wise mentors. Solitary visions are unsafe; I invite correction.
3. Fruit. If it yields love, repentance, holiness, and service, I keep it; if not, I discard it.
4. Time. Truth strengthens with waiting; falsehood withers. I do not rush major decisions.
5. Sobriety. Grace does not fear psychology. I examine trauma patterns and triggers honestly—and seek clinical input when needed.
6. Ordinary obedience. Genuine experiences send me back to prayer, sacraments, fellowship, and service—not away from them.
7. No new doctrine. Christ is the final Word; nothing I see adds to that.

APPENDIX: GUARDRAILS / MENTAL HEALTH HELPLINES

8. Peace over pressure. The Spirit convicts without coercion. If an "impression" demands secrecy, shames others, or bypasses conscience, I set it aside.

9. Boundaries. Any "word" that asks for money, isolation, or special access is rejected and reported.

MENTAL HEALTH HELPLINES

If you are carrying wounds from abuse:

- Immediate danger: call emergency services.
- Need to talk now: reach out to a trusted crisis helpline in your country.
- Clerical/spiritual abuse: contact independent survivor-advocacy groups and safeguarding offices not tied to the alleged abuser.
- Document and report: preserve messages/evidence; seek legal/medical care as appropriate; do not confront an abuser alone.
- For church leaders: believe disclosures; do not promise secrecy; follow local law and report to authorities; remove accused persons from ministry during investigation; protect children and the vulnerable above reputation.

If anyone is in immediate danger, use the local emergency number (e.g., 999/911/112). In the EU, 112 works in every member state.

UNITED STATES

- 988 Suicide and Crisis Lifeline: call/text 988; chat at 988lifeline.org.

APPENDIX: GUARDRAILS / MENTAL HEALTH HELPLINES

- RAINN National Sexual Assault Hotline: 800-656-HOPE (4673).
- National Domestic Violence Hotline: 800-799-SAFE (7233); text START to 88788.

CANADA

- 9-8-8 Suicide Crisis Helpline: call/text 988.
- Kids Help Phone: 800-668-6868; text 686868 (youth / young adults).

UNITED KINGDOM

- Samaritans: 116 123 (free, 24/7 emotional support).
- Refuge: 0808 2000 247 (national domestic abuse helpline).
- Rape Crisis England and Wales: 0808 500 2222 (24/7 support line).

EUROPEAN UNION / EEA (COUNTRY AVAILABILITY MAY VARY)

- EU Emergency: 112 (police/ambulance/fire, any member state).
- Emotional Support Helpline: 116 123 (where active).
- Victims of Crime Helpline: 116 006 (where active).
- Child Helpline: 116 111 (where active).

Appendix: Guardrails / Mental Health Helplines

AUSTRALIA

- Lifeline: 13 11 14 (crisis support / suicide prevention).
- 1800RESPECT: 1800 737 732 (domestic, family, and sexual violence).

NEW ZEALAND

- 1737, Need to Talk?: call/text 1737 (national mental health, 24/7).
- Safe to Talk: 0800 044 334; text 4334 (sexual harm helpline).
- Women's Refuge: 0800 REFUGE / 0800 733 843 (24/7 crisis).
- Shine: 0508 744 633 (family violence).

INDIA

- Emergency: 112 (all-in-one emergency number; standard nationwide).
- KIRAN: 1800-599-0019 (national mental health helpline, 24/7).
- Tele MANAS (MoHFW Mental Health): 14416 (24/7).
- CHILDLINE: 1098 (children in distress, 24/7).
- Women's Helpline: 181 (state-run access to services; availability by state).
- iCALL (TISS Counseling): 9152987821 / 022-25521111 (hours vary).

APPENDIX: GUARDRAILS / MENTAL HEALTH HELPLINES

AFRICA

- SADAG Suicide Crisis Line: 0800 567 567 (South Africa, 24/7).
- Continent-Wide Directories (find your country's number):
  » Befrienders Worldwide: befrienders.org (suicide support).
  » Find a Helpline: findahelpline.com (verified crisis lines).

ASIA (OUTSIDE INDIA)

- Use these verified directories to get the correct number for each country:
  » Befrienders Worldwide: befrienders.org (suicide/emotional support).
  » Find a Helpline: findahelpline.com (suicide, DV, sexual abuse, more).

Attila Takacs is a Jewish-Christian writer whose work explores trauma, mercy, and the fierce tenderness of God. Born in Hungary and now based in Scotland, he brings a distinctive voice shaped by both ancient tradition and lived experience. His writing blends prophetic clarity with pastoral compassion, inviting readers to see holiness in unexpected places.

@OFFICIALLY_ATTY

www.ingramcontent.com/pod-product-compliance
Lightning Source LLC
Chambersburg PA
CBHW071712040426
42446CB00011B/2031